SPIR'IT-UAL
AR'CHI-TEC'TURE

CHRISTIAN LaSALLE WALDEN

"Some people are trying to live in the blessings of the Lord while still talking like the devil."

Opening Remarks

To those people in my life who have so skillfully used the game of power to manipulate, torture, and cause me pain over the years, I bear you no grudges and I thank you for supplying me with inspiration and motivation.

"Jesus + Anything = Nothing
Jesus + Nothing = Everything"
James P. Gills, MD

Dedication

This book is dedicated to my grandmother Carola Landis Rice. Prophetess Rice was my inspiration to write this novel. She has shown continued appreciation for her Master through tremendous trials. Carola, thank you for being a 1 Thessalonians 5:16-22 kind of woman. "Be joyful always; pray continually; give thanks in all circumstances, for this is God's will for you in Christ Jesus. Don't try to stop what the Holy Spirit is doing. Don't treat prophecies as if they weren't important. But test all prophesies. Say no to every kind of evil." You have given all of us a gorgeous example of how to undergo trials that have made you a greater and stronger woman in Christ. Thank you for being such an encouraging and uplifting; Grandmother, Mother, Daughter, Aunt; a true warrior for God.

May we challenge each other to live this life of joy, romance, and an adventurous mystery in abandoning ourselves to the grace of God so that we may be thrilled with Him both now and forever. Thank you, FuFu for giving us a living example of the grace of God and the joy of the Lord as the believer's strength.

Table of Contents

I.

Acknowledgements

I would like to acknowledge my indebtedness to my family, close friends and supporters who have shown me so many truths. I have seen daily that my greatest sin of omission is my lack of appreciation; and my greatest sin of commission is worrying about things that are not realities.

I am also thankful for people such as: Regina Reed, my right hand woman of God and also my mother. My right hand man and my blood brother Darius Brown. Of course, the beautiful woman I dedicated this book to, and also my grandmother (FuFu) Carola Rice.

Last but certainly not least, my gorgeous son Hayden. Son, there's not one second of the day you don't cross my mind. You motivate and inspire me every single day to be the best father I can be.

Also, special thanks to those who have never left my side; family and friends, you know who you are; may God continue to bless you all.

II.

Help in the Time of Need

~ The Way of Salvation (John 14:6, Acts 16:31, Romans 10:9)

~ Comfort In The Time of Loneliness (Psalms 23, Deuteronomy 31:6, Matthew 28:20, Isaiah 41:10)

~ Comfort In Time of Sorrow (Deuteronomy 34:8, Isaiah 53: 4-6)

~ Relief In Time of Suffering (2 Corinthians 1:3-5, Hebrews 4:16)

~ Guidance In Time of Decision (James 1:5-6, Proverbs 3: 5-6)

~ Protection In Time of Danger (Psalms 91, 121:8)

~ Courage In Time of Fear (Psalm 34-4, Isaiah 41:10, Proverbs 29-25)

~ Peace In Time of Turmoil (Jude 1:2, Philippians 4: 6-9)

~ Rest In Time of Weariness (Matthew 11: 28-29)

~ Strength In Time of Temptation (James 1:12-16, 1 Corinthians 10:6-13)

~ Warning In Time of Indifference (Galatians 5:19-21, Hebrews 10:26-31)

~ Forgiveness In Time of Conviction (Isaiah 1:18, 1 John 1:7-9)

III.

Foreword by Prophetess Carola L. Rice

For everything there is a season and for every season there is a reason and a purpose. From the depths of my soul, I find great joy in supporting my grandson, Christian LaSalle Walden in his endeavor to follow in the footsteps of his FuFu by writing his first book. I stand in awe of what God is doing with my seed. My War Room experience(s) with my Savior has proven to me that every promise He has  spoken is real. He promised to keep my seed even in the midst of their own circumstances. The heartfelt love and prayers along with the mighty spirit of an awesome God has developed a young man, Christian into a man that God is calling to serve Him with all that he is, has and will receive. With many tears and constant prayer, I trusted my God to see him through; and He has. I stood, demanding the enemy to leave my family alone.

Christian LaSalle Walden belongs to God; and it was God that I would feed him, and to lead him to the place where he would meet Him and then run on to his victory. So, my beloved grandson, run on with King Jesus; and you will never run or walk alone.

Love you always Christian,
Your FuFu

IV.

Foreword by Pastor Jacqueline M. White

As stated in Genesis 1:1 in the King James translation of the Holy Bible, "In the beginning God created the heaven and the earth"; and further, in verses 27-28, "So God created man in his own image...male and female created he them. And God blessed them, and God said unto them, Be fruitful, and multiply, and replenish the earth, and subdue it: and have dominion over the fish of the sea, and over the fowl of the air, and over every living thing that moveth upon the earth." But in the journey of life, there are challenges that often cause us to take a different trail than that intended by God; thus rendering our true destinies dormant or unrealized. However, I believe the old adage, "A delay is not always a denial."

When your bones have been dried too long, it is time to come out of that "dry place". In this Scripture, Job 23:10 portrays a man acquainted with disappointment, sorrow and calamity who learns to hold onto faith and thrust his way to triumph. His latter became greater than his beginnings. Job himself declares in that same scripture, "But he knoweth the way I take: when he hath tried me, I shall come forth as gold."

From the day of his birth, June 18, 1993, I have known this author, Christian LaSalle Walden, who is my great-nephew. His life path, though shaken, has not gone unnoticed. Undoubtedly, he can make the same declaration as the Apostle Paul, an author of biblical scripture, who maintained his probity despite his many tribulations; and who wrote in Ephesians 3:20, "Now unto him that is able to do exceeding abundantly above all that we ask or think, according to the power that worketh in us,…" recognizing that regardless of the gravity of one's life situation, God is still in control.

Through his masterminded message, *Ar'chi-tec'ture*, the author reveals the fact that understanding the heart of God can bring life, even to situations that appear the most futile. The reader will experience a spiritual awakening and learn that failures are not necessarily fatal. Christian's desire is to share the revelation that God's plan is the best plan for your life. Proverbs 3:3-4 reads "Let not mercy and truth forsake thee: bind them about thy neck; write them upon the table of thine heart: So shalt thou find favour and good understanding in the sight of God and man."

I pray that each reader will feel Christian's very heartbeat. Nothing binds God or moves Him like a solemn covenant; that is one made from the heart and entered into through faith!

Jacqueline M. White, Pastor and Apostle
Powerhouse Church of God, Lexington, Kentucky
(powerhousechurchofgod.org)
Author, *Slaughtered Sheep*

V.

Foreword by Minister Vivian C. Fields

It was such an honor and a surprise to me when I received a request from Christian LaSalle Walden to write a foreword for his upcoming new release of Spir'it-ual Ar'chi-tec'ture. Now, you have to look at the spelling of the title to understand what Christian is trying to say and how he is trying to relay his story, so that it will have the spiritual impact on the lives of those who will find themselves in this Ark which in Hebrew the word Tebah means a box or chest, a place of refuge for those stored within it.

I have known Christian LaSalle Walden every since he was born. He has always been a well mannered young man that was very intellectual and articulate. Christian was no stranger to God, for he was co-raised by a highly favored and anointed grandmother, prophetess and Author Carola Landis Rice. Yet Christian had not experienced an intimate relationship with God, but the events that would take place later in his young adult life would assuredly catapult him into a place where he would seek the God of refuge. False accusations of a love gone bad causing his first debut before a merciless Judge that would make him an example for other young black men. As a first time offender, injustice rang loud as a jury of his peers found him guilty, but what the devil meant for bad God meant it for his good.

While incarcerated in several Georgia correctional facilities, the Ar'chi-tec'ture layout would provide the best comfort for Christian as the enemy preys upon his mind to destroy his life by speaking death by attempted suicide and constant fear would war within to only give way to the divine light of the Ark. What may have looked like defeat for him now becomes not just a testimony to share but a transformation illuminated by the power and spirit of a forgiving and loving God. Christian LaSalle Walden was now a layout in the plan of God to be used as his instrument to encourage others that no matter what you're facing in life, God is the Spir'-it-ual Ar'ki-tek'tur of your soul; and He will complete a great work in you if you let Him.

VI.

Introduction

I'm convinced that the cause of many of life's failures, shortcomings, and downfalls is that we, as human beings, lack gratitude and appreciation for our Master. As a result of taking His precious gift of life for granted, we live in discontent and misery, complaining about what we don't have and failing to express genuine appreciation for what we do have.

I am also highly convinced that by simply stopping to appreciate the world around us, as well as the marvelous "world" of life within us – our human body – our whole perspective of this thing we call life can be transformed better than we could ever imagine. Once I put everything and everyone living in the flesh behind me, and decided to walk with God; my life changed forever. Thank you for taking the time out to read my novel; and may God Bless you all.

Blueprint ONE

Why is Human Life So (Valuable)?

They lived in the deepest darkness. They suffered as prisoners in iron chains. They tripped and fell, and there was no one to help them. Then they cried out to the Lord because of their problems. And He saved them from their troubles. He brought them out of the deepest darkness. He broke their chains off. He breaks down gates that are made of bronze. He cuts through bars that are made of iron. He made the storm as quiet as a whisper. The waves of the ocean calmed down. Let them give thanks to the Lord for His faithful love. Let them give thanks for the wonderful things He does for His people.

Perhaps you have spent some time sitting in darkness.

Perhaps you are familiar with gloom.

Perhaps you have felt like there is no one to help you.

Maybe you have given up all hope – for you, for your life, for anything. God can break into your darkness. God can help you break out of your deepest misery. God can break into your darkness. God can help you break out of your deepest misery. God can do this for you, but will you accept Him? If you will turn to God and honestly bring him your questions, He will answer. Go to your Creator and ask Him for help.

Psalm 69 quotes, "God save me. My troubles are like a flood. I'm up to my neck in them. I'm sinking in deep mud. I have no firm place to stand. I am out in deep water. The waves roll over me. I'm worn out from calling for help. My throat is very dry. My eyes grow tired looking for my God.

You may be asking, "How does He do it?" He comes near to you. He is not afraid to pour His love right into the middle of your life. God hears your cry for help. He has already sent you an answer. He sends forth His Word to heal you. Every person is created in God's image. God carefully made each one of us. He knows each of us very well. The Creator Himself gives us life. God even sent His Son Jesus Christ to become like us so we would not lose His gift of life forever.

"You created the deepest parts of my being. You put me together inside my mother's womb. How you made me is amazing and wonderful. I praise you for that. What you have done is wonderful. I know that very well. None of my bones was hidden from you when you made me inside my mother's womb. That place was as dark as the deepest parts of the earth. When you were putting me together there, your eyes saw my body even before it was formed. You planned how many days I would live. You wrote down the number of them in your book before I had lived through even one of them. God, your thoughts about me are priceless."

I'd be falsifying the truth if I said that I understood and was thankful for the true value of life growing up. As an adolescent, I would get upset if I didn't get things I "wanted". See, there's a huge difference between a "want" and a "need", which we all know. We as human's, greed for things that just really don't matter. It wasn't until when I found God, until I started understanding that something non-materialistic such as taking the next breath was the true value of life. Life is taken for granted, and we don't really pay attention to the bigger picture, which is falling in love with Christ first and then finding your Father, God. The only way to the King is through the Son. When you finally choose to walk alongside with your Master, everything you could ever desire will pour down on you overwhelmingly, which we call blessings. "Some people are trying to live in the blessings of the Lord while still talking like the devil".

Spir'it-ual Ar'ki-tek'tur is a book about building a relationship with our Master. Our job as His children is to find Him, and bring the blind to Him. God wants you to receive His free gift of salvation. Jesus wants to save you and fill you with the Holy Spirit more than anything. If you have never invited Jesus, the Prince of Peace, to be your Lord and Savior, I invite you to do so now. One of a few favors I'm going to ask of you throughout my teachings is that you, the reader, pray the following prayer, and if you are really sincere about it, you will experience a new life in Christ. Here's a prayer for a personal relationship with the Lord. "Father, You loved the world so much, You gave Your only begotten Son to die for our sins so that whoever believed in Him will not perish, but have eternal life."

Your Word says we are saved by grace through faith as a gift from You. There is nothing we can do to earn salvation. I believe and confess with my mouth that Jesus Christ is Your Son, the Savior of the World. I believe He died on the cross for me and bore all of my sins, paying the price for them. I believe in my heart that You raised Jesus from the dead. I ask You to forgive my sins. I confess Jesus as my Lord. According to Your Word, I am saved and will spend eternity with You. Thank you, Father...I am so grateful; in Jesus' name, Amen. Respond to God in prayer. As you pray, you are free to tell God all of the things that concern you. As you read in the Bible what concerns Him.

In Response:
- Take the time to respond to what you have read
- Thank Him for His promises

- Be responsive to the changes the Holy Spirit wants you to make
- Confess your sins
- Thank God that you are learning more and more what God is truly like
- Ask Him for a deeper, clearer understanding of what a passage means and how it can help you to become more like Jesus.

Relationships are built through communication, and two-way communication is better communication.

Note section for readers
WRITE IT DOWN–Keep a written record of what you discover when you spend time reading God's Word and praying. Your journal will help you see how you are growing in faith. It will help you remember what you have learned and will keep it fresh in your mind so that you can continue to be influenced by it for the rest of the day. Building a relationship is not easy. It requires discipline, communication, patience, trust, and time. A relationship with God is no exception. Spend time with Him in His Word and in prayer. Take your conversation with Him into every part of your daily life. Allow Him to speak to you and take time, often, to speak with Him. As you do, your life with God will develop and deepen, and, as it does, you will find that the results are well worth the effort.

_____

_____

_____

_____

Blueprint TWO

What is the (Purpose) for my Life?

The only way to find the true purpose for your life is to give your life to God's purpose. The reason you exist is to serve the One who made you. Many people try to create their own meaning in life, but this will always fail. Only the good and loving plans of God will last.

Colossians 1:9 states, "We keep asking God to fill you with the knowledge of what He wants. We pray He will give you the wisdom and understanding that the Spirit gives. Then you will be able to lead a life that is worthy of the Lord. We pray that you will please Him in every way. So we want you to bear fruit in every good thing you do. We pray that you will grow to know God better. We want you to be very strong, in keeping with His glorious power. We want you to be patient. We pray that you will never give up. We want you to give thanks with joy to the Father. He has made you fit to have what He will give to all His holy people. You will all receive a share in the kingdom of light".

Paul states clearly that all things in heaven and earth were created through Jesus. All things were brought back to God by Jesus' death on the cross. Jesus Christ is the fullness of God's being. Paul tells the Colossians that belief in Jesus Christ is all they need to be saved. God has made them into new people. So now they can live their faith to the fullest. Nothing needs to be added to it. Paul ends his letter with practical advice on how to live the new life of following Jesus.

You have been raised up with Christ. So think about things that are in heaven. That is where Christ is. He is sitting at God's right hand. Think about things that are in heaven Don't think about things that are only on earth. Christ is your life. When He appears again, you also will appear with Him in heaven's glory. So put to death anything that comes from sinful desires. Get rid of sexual sins and impure acts. Don't let your feelings get out of control. Remove from your life all evil desires–stop always wanting more and more. You might as well be worshipping statues of god's.

God's anger is going to come because of these things. That's the way you lived at one time in your life, but now here are the kinds of things you must also get rid of. You must get rid of anger, rage, hate and lies. Let no dirty words come out of your mouths. Don't lie to one another. You have gotten rid of your old way of life and its habits. You have started living a new life. Your knowledge of how that life should have the Creator's likeness is being made new.

We, as humans tend to stress about our purpose in life. I, myself, was the same until I started to spend alone time with God. Many fear even being alone and in most cases it is not a good thing. If you're anything like myself, your mind starts to race, and we all know that an idle mind is the devil's playground. But, this is not quite the alone time I'm trying to touch on.

The best time to connect with your Creator is when you're by yourself with no distractions. When you are able to open your mind and heart, and just start praying to your Father and sincerely mean it without being selfish, He will start blessing you through signs. This is how you find your true purpose in life. The Lord will send signs through other people that have a genuine relationship with Him. Trust me, I'm a living witness. Let the peace that Christ gives rule in your hearts. As parts of one body, you were appointed to live in peace and be thankful. Let the message from God, no matter what type of sign it comes from, live among you like a rich treasure.

Anyone who loves their life will lose it; but anyone who hates their life in this world will keep it and have eternal life. Anyone who serves Me must follow Me. And where I am, my servant will also be. My Father will honor the one who serves Me – John 12:26.

At this point, you may be asking yourself, "What happens now?" Jesus will now be your leader. You will now live for Him and for His kingdom; and the power of His love and forgiveness is spreading all around the world. Not everything will change at once, but Jesus Christ will stay with you. His Holy Spirit is already working in your life. The Spirit will help you keep growing in knowledge, faith, and obedience. I am no saint; and I'm not saying that things will be easy. You will have hard times and problems. It will take strength to keep on following Jesus. But, you also know for sure that even now Jesus is bringing all of history to God's final purpose.

There is no question whatsoever about the outcome. His kingdom is coming, and one day all people will see that Jesus is the world's true Lord and Ruler. You can show your commitment to Jesus by faithfully following Him right now. This is why Jesus is also your hope. His followers wait for the time He will finish the work He has started. God will come down and make His home with us. There will be a renewed heaven and earth; and this will be our ultimate healing.

"In the book of Revelation, chapter 21:3, it states; God now makes His home with the people. He will live with them; they will be His people, and God Himself will be with them and be their God. He will wipe away every tear from their eyes. There will be no more death, and there will be no more sadness; there will be no more crying or pain. Things are no longer the way they used to be."

Note section for readers

WRITE IT DOWN

_____

_____

_____

_____

_____

_____

_____

_____

_____

_____

Blueprint THREE

How do I live as a follower of Jesus?

Part I: Clean living in an unclean world

L et's start with God's answer to stone-hearted hearts. God's love is greater than our problems, so God told His people that He would fix this problem of sin-hardened hearts. God Himself made amazing promises to change them from the inside out. Ezekiel 36:24 tells us "I will take you out of the nations. I will gather you together from all the countries. I will bring you back into your own land. I will sprinkle pure water on you; then you will be 'clean'. I will make you completely pure and 'clean'. I will take all the statues of your gods away from you. I will give you new hearts. I will give you a new spirit that is faithful to Me. I will remove your stubborn hearts from you. I will give you hearts that obey Me. I will put my spirit in you. I will make you want to obey My rules. I want you to be careful to keep My laws; then you will live in the land I gave your people of long ago. You will be My people, and I will be your God."

God made good on these promises when Jesus dies on a cross; and put sin to death. If you have joined with Jesus Christ, you have had your hard old heart changed from the inside. Because Jesus Christ rose from the dead, God gave you a new life and a new heart as well. So, don't let sin rule your body, which is going to die. Don't obey its evil desires. Don't let any part of yourself be used to do evil. Instead, give yourselves to God. You have been brought from death to life. So give every part of yourself to God to do what is right. Sin will no longer control you like a master; that's because the law does not rule you. God's grace has already set you free – Romans 6:15-23.

I'm hoping we're making some progress here. Here's a message to God's new people. God's people are now free to know the blessing of living by God's laws. The followers of Jesus have the power of Jesus; and the help of the Holy Spirit. They can set their hearts and minds on that God really wants. Christ died for everyone. He died so that those who live should not live for themselves anymore; they should live for Christ. He died for them and was raised again.

So from now on we don't look at anyone the way the world does. At one time we looked at Christ in that way. But, we don't anymore. When anyone lives in Christ, the new creation has come – the old is gone. The new is here. All this is from God. He brought us back to Himself through Christ's death on the Cross; and He has given us the task of bringing others back to Him through Christ – 2 Corinthians 5.

Remember, the only way to the Heavenly Father is through His only beloved Son, Jesus Christ – always keep this in mind. Now, pay close attention to God's law for today. Jesus knew and loved the law God had given His people in the Old Testament. Jesus also knew how to get to the very heart of the law.

The Pharisees heard that the Sadducees weren't able to answer Jesus. So the Pharisees got together. One of them was an authority on the law. So he tested Jesus with a question. "Teacher, he asked, which is the most important commandment in the Law?" Jesus replied, "Love the Lord your God with all your heart and with all your soul. Love Him with all your mind. This is the first and most important commandment. And the second is like it, "Love your neighbor as you love yourself."

Everything that is written in the Law and the Prophets is based on these two commandments." – Matthew 22:34.

God has two main things to say about how He wants His followers to live: 1) Love God with everything you have, and 2) Love each other with a deep, self-giving kind of love. Do not be hard-hearted toward God or others. These two greatest of all laws are also the greatest of all loves.

The greatest Commandment is loving God with everything. God has loved his people greatly – rescuing them from danger and trouble, even from sin and death; and, He wants His people to love Him greatly in return. This means giving God the highest place in your life, making service to Jesus the most essential thing.

In the Old Testament, God's people had many nations all around them. These nations believed their own gods could protect and provide for them. God's people were always being tempted to trust and serve these other gods. But God's Word tells us that people from all around the world will finally see that these fake gods always fail.

"Our people of long ago didn't own anything except statues of gods; the statues were worthless. They didn't do them any good. Do human beings really make their own gods? Yes; but they aren't really gods at all."

The Lord says, "So I will teach them about myself. This time I will show them how powerful and mighty I am; then, they will know that I am the Lord." – Jeremiah 16:21.

Today, the followers of Jesus are also tempted to trust in false gods. It is easy to believe that enough money will solve all out problems. We quickly start to depend on our own strength. Often, we foolishly follow the directions of the world; and then we pay the painful results. In the end, the idols of today's world have nothing to offer.

Here is what people who belong to this world do:

- They try to satisfy what their sinful desires want to do
- They long for what their sinful eyes look at
- They take pride in what they have and what they do

All of this comes from the world. None of it comes from the Father. The world and its evil desires are passing away; but whoever does what God wants them to do lives forever – 1 John 2:17.

The followers of Jesus have been set free from slavery to the false gods. How much better will it be to give ourselves to the Lord of lord's and King of kings. This kind of commitment to God results in our entire lives becoming special gifts to God. It means loving God through our work, our rest, our play, our family, our friendships, our thoughts, our worship and with everything we own. It means loving God with everything we say, think and do. It means living our lives the way we were meant to, the way our Creator intended; followers of Jesus who live to love God.

The second greatest commandment is loving your neighbor deeply. The good news of the kingdom of God is for everyone. So Jesus calls His followers from everywhere – from all around the world, from all sorts of cultures, from all races of people, and from all social classes. We should not expect every follower of Jesus to be the same.

Sometimes the wonderful differences in the body of Christ are turned into terrible divisions. Differences in skin color or denomination or nationality have led to countless conflicts. But it is wrong to make the ways in which we are different more important than the faith we share in Jesus. The Bible says we are one.

Don't be proud at all. Be completely gentle. Be patient. Put up with one another in love. The Holy Spirit makes you one in every way. So try your best to remain as one. Let peace keep you together. There is one body and one Spirit. You were appointed to one hope when you were chosen. There is one Lord, one faith and one baptism. There is one God and Father of all. He is over everything. He is through everything. He is in everything – Ephesians 4.

The second greatest love comes from the first. The Son of God loved us even to the point of giving up His life. As disciples of the Son we follow His example day by day. We deny ourselves and love each other deeply. We have the new commandment of love written on our hearts. This love is not a weakness; it is the tough, passionate love that really cares about others. It is the love that is strong enough to step forward and help people.

Note section for readers

WRITE IT DOWN

_____

_____

_____

_____

_____

_____

_____

Blueprint Four

How do I live as a follower of Jesus?

Part 2: Be part of the Body

Not alone, but together. When we decide to follow Jesus, we become members of God's family. All Christians are adopted into this family. The followers of Jesus are not people who stay by themselves in their walk with the Lord. God's salvation produces a new community – the people of God.

But God chose you to be His people. You are royal priests. You are a holy nation. You are God's special treasure. You are all these things so that you can give Him praise. God brought you out of darkness into His wonderful light. Once, you were a lost people; but, now you are no longer lost, now the people of God. Once you had not received mercy; but, now you have received mercy – 1Peter 2:9-10. This new gathering of people is called the body of Christ – read 1Corinthians 12:27.

What will I find when I join with God's people? Life in God's kingdom is life together everlasting. Do not try to walk alone with Jesus. Find other followers of Jesus and meet regularly with them. When the body of Christ gathers, there is joy in sharing, music, prayer, teaching, and worship. Your task for the day is to read Romans 12 to learn more about this. You can also expect to find:

A Place to Belong

As members of God's family, the followers of Jesus come together by God's spirit. Here is a place you can know that you really belong. Here is where you can find support, encouragement, and real friendship. God Himself welcomes you into this household of faith. So, you are no longer strangers and outsiders; you are citizens together with God's people. You are members of God's family.

A Place to Serve

The spiritual body of Christ works together like a physical body. Each member of Christ's body has a special purpose and job. You can find the special gifts God has given you by serving others. Soon, you will see which gifts God has given you. Mark my words; we all serve a purpose both now and forever.

A Place to be Served

The different parts of the body depend on each other. As you serve others, you in turn will find God using others to meet your needs. God wants us to know the blessing of supporting each other.

A Place to Grow

Just as your physical body needs food, so too your spiritual life needs to be fed. Jesus Christ wants you to grow and mature in your faith, your spiritual life and your service. The spiritual food you need includes teaching from God's Word, sharing with other believers, and prayer and praise to God.

A Place to Obey

The Christian faith is personal, but not private. Healthy and growing followers of Jesus are not loners. It is by living in community with others that you test how well you obey the great command of love.

Jesus called them together. He said, "You know about those who are rulers of the Gentiles. They hold power over their people. Their high officials order them around – Mark 10:42.

Don't be like that. Instead, anyone who wants to be first must be the slave of everyone. Even the son of man did not come to be served. Instead, he came to serve others. He came to give his life as the price for setting many people free." – Matthew 20:28

Jesus Prays for All Believers

"I do not pray only for them alone. I also pray for everyone who will believe in Me because of their message." Father, I pray they will be one, just as You are in Me and I am in You. I want them also to be in us; then the world will believe that You have sent Me. I have given them glory you gave Me. I did this so they would be one, just as we are one. I will be in them, just as You are in Me. This is so that they may be brought together perfectly as one. Then the world will know that you sent Me. It will also show the world that you have loved those You gave Me, just as You have loved Me. "Father, I want those You have given Me to be with Me where I am. I want them to see My glory, the glory You have given Me. You gave it to Me because you loved Me before the world was created. Father, You are holy. The world does not know You, but I know You. Those You have given Me know You have sent Me. I have shown You to them; and I will continue to show You to them. Then the love You have for Me will be in them. I myself will be in them." – John 17:20-26

Note section for readers

WRITE IT DOWN

_____

_____

_____

_____

_____

_____

_____

_____

_____

_____

_____

Blueprint Five

How can I get over my Anger/Temper?

Listen folks, I'm not saying that we always have to be happy-go-lucky all the time. I get it; we're only human. Your anger is not always wrong. After all, God certainly gets angry when we hurt each other and Him. God gets angry about injustice; and Jesus got angry when He was on earth. Perhaps you are angry at someone who cheated you, or someone who betrayed you. Maybe you are upset at some real wrongs.

But the problem with our anger is that we so often do the wrong thing with it. Does your anger ever take on a life of its own, out of your control? Then it becomes harmful and evil. Often it backfires, causing you more pain than the problem that caused it. Anger often leads to sin. This leads to more anger and then you may want to get even and hurt others.

God chose to give us new birth through the message of truth. He wanted us to be the first harvest of His new creation. My dear brothers and sisters; pay attention to what I say. Everyone should be quick to listen; and slow to speak. They should be slow to get angry. Human anger doesn't produce the holy life God wants for us.

In the book of Ephesians, Chapter 4 verse 26, the scripture says, "When you are angry, do not sin". Do not let the sun go down while you are still angry. Don't give the devil a chance. Don't let any evil talk come out of your mouths. Say only what will help to build others up and meet their needs. Then what you say will help those who listen. Do not make God's Holy Spirit mourn. The Holy Spirit is the proof that you belong to God. And the Spirit is the proof that God will set you completely free. Get rid of all hard feelings, anger and rage. Stop the fighting and lying. Don't have anything to do with any kind of hatred. Be kind and tender to one another, just as God forgave you because of what Christ has done. You are the children that God dearly loves.

So follow His example. Lead a life of love, just as Christ did. He loved us. He gave Himself up for us. He was a sweet-smelling offering and sacrifice to God. From now on, make up your mind to think about your anger when you feel it coming on. First, decide if you really have a good reason to be angry. Next, think about how to use it properly. Do not use your anger to do more harm. Harming others with malicious intent is not Christ-like. Let God's peace and God's power fill you instead and you will reign supreme in every situation.

Note section for readers

WRITE IT DOWN

_____

_____

_____

_____

Blueprint Six

How do I live as a follower of Jesus?

Part 3: Visiting hours with God

Moses led God's people into an awful trap. They were surrounded. On one side was the ocean and on the other was an army that wanted to kill them. Moses prayed desperately and God split the sea so they could escape. Another time, the Apostle Peter was in prison, chained up and guarded by sixteen men. The night before he was to be sentenced, an angel of the Lord visited him. This angel broke through Peter's chain and walked him right past the guards.

Peter's friends were so surprised when he knocked on their door that they forgot to answer it. They had been praying for him, but when they saw him they thought Peter's ghost had interrupted their all night prayer service. One of the amazing things about prayer is how powerful it is. God hears us when we pray, even if we're not exactly sure how we should do it. Before He left His disciples, Jesus talked to them about prayer:

"Now it's your time to be sad. But I will see you again. Then you will be full of joy. And no one will take away your joy."

"When that day comes, you will no longer ask Me for anything. What I'm about to tell you is true. My Father will give you anything you ask for in My name. Ask, and you will receive what you ask for. Then your joy will be complete."

"I have not been speaking to you plainly. But a time is coming when I will speak clearly. Then I will tell you plainly about my Father. When that day comes, you will ask for things in my name. I am not saying I will ask the Father instead of you asking Him. No, the Father Himself loves you because you have loved Me. He also loves you because you have believed that I came from God." – John 16:25

Prayer is one of the deepest, most mysterious things a Christian can do. Prayer must have priority. Prayer must be our bolt to lock up the night, our key to open the day. – James P. Gills, MD

Some aspects of it are always true:

1. God always wants us to pray, for ourselves and for others.

   The Bible is full of prayers. People prayed for themselves, for those they cared for and for those they had never even met.

   God helps us know what to pray for. Throughout the day He sends His spirit to point out different ways for us to pray. It's almost as if the Holy Spirit taps on our shoulder and points to some place the Lord is working. We can thank God for something, ask for His help or invite Him to join us in whatever we're doing. We can pray for God's bigger purposes in the world. We can pray for His kingdom. If you're still not sure how to do it, read a prayer and note what the person who prayed it said. Try this with the following passages: Luke 11, Psalm 51, Ephesians 3, and Ezra 9

   We have the Holy Spirit as the promise of future blessing. But we also groan inside ourselves. We do this as we look forward to the time when God adopts us full members of His family. Then He will give us everything He has for us. He will raise our bodies and give glory to them.

That's the hope we had when we were saved. But hope that can be seen is no hope at all. Who hopes for what they already have? We hope for what we don't have yet. So we are patient as we wait for it. In the same way, the Holy Spirit helps us when we are weak. We don't know what we should pray for. But the Spirit Himself prays for us. He rays through groans too deep for words. God, who looks into our hearts, knows the mind of the Spirit. And the Spirit prays for God's people; just as God wants him to pray. – Romans 8

2. God wants to amaze us with His awesome power.

Prayer joins human effort with God's power. One person can change the world if he only understands God's plan for it and prays. For more than three years not a drop of rain had fallen. God told His prophet Elijah to gather all His people together. For many months these people had been begging their false gods for rain. Now it was time for the people to make a choice.

Elijah told them to prepare an offering to their gods while he prepared an offering to the living God. He then killed a bull, cut it up and spread the piece s on a pile of wood. While the huge crowd was crying out to their gods, Elijah poured bucket after bucket of water on his offering pile.

At the end of the day, when the other gods had still not responded, Elijah called out to the living God. Immediately the fire of the Lord came down from heaven and burned up the sacrifice. And for the first time in three years the sky suddenly grew dark and it began to rain. Read more of this amazing story in 1 Kings 18.

God wants you to be someone who causes great things to happen on earth. Read these passages to see how God showed his awesome power to other people: Isaiah 38, Psalm 145, 2 Samuel 7:22, Paul's letters to the Philippians and 2 Corinthians.

3. God wants us to praise Him and thank Him.

   The Old Testament prophet Daniel got caught praying. For his punishment he got thrown into a den with some hungry lions. Daniel started to pray. Early the next morning the king who had put Daniel in the lion's den hurried to see how he was.

   Daniel told the king, "My God sent His angel. And His angel shut the mouths of the lions. "Amazed, the king sent a letter to people all across his empire, ordering them to respect and honor Daniel's God. People praised God in every language for his miracle.

   Daniel probably prayed for safety that night. And like Daniel we all have things we want from God. But what has God already given you or done for you that you can thank Him for?

   Sometimes we find ourselves in a room full of lions. Thanking God for what's happening is the last thing we feel like doing. But thanking God for the difficult unpleasant events shows we trust Him.

   Read these passages for ideas on how to praise God and than Him: 1 Samuel 2, Psalm 100, 103, and Luke 1.

The Final Word –

God knows what's happening to you, what you're thinking and what you need, no matter where you are. He wants you to turn your thoughts toward Him throughout the day. He longs for you to ask Him for help – for yourself, for the people around you, for the world. He wants to visit with you, right where you are now. Brothers and sisters, we are not afraid to enter the most Holy Room. We enter boldly because of the blood of Jesus. His way is new because He lives. It has been opened for us through the curtain. I'm talking about his body.

We also have a great priest over the house of God. So let us come near to God with a sincere heart. Let us come near boldly because of our faith. Our hearts have been sprinkled. Our minds have been cleansed from a sense of guilt. Our bodies have been washed with pure water.

Let us hold firmly to the hope we claim to have. The God who promised is faithful. – Hebrews 10

Note section for readers

WRITE IT DOWN

_____

_____

_____

_____

_____

_____

_____

_____

Blueprint Seven

How do I live as a follower of Jesus?

Part 4: Fight the Spiritual Battle

To all my followers of Jesus Christ and our Heavenly Father, fighting the spiritual battle is the real war. When you become a follower of Jesus, you take sides in a battle. You are now involved in the real struggle of the universe. Satan will try to make you useless to God and his kingdom.

You will find powerful weapons used against you: lies, temptations, fears and perhaps even physical violence. You cannot fight this battle with the weapons of the world. The real war is on a different level.

Located in our Holy Bible, here's how the early Christian leader Paul describes our spiritual battle:

Finally, let the Lord make you strong. Depend on His mighty power. Put on all of God's armor. Then you can remain strong against the devil's evil plans. Our fight is not against human beings. It is against the rulers, the authorities and the powers of this dark world. It is against the spiritual forces of evil in the heavenly world.

The Final Word –

God knows what's happening to you, what you're thinking and what you need, no matter where you are. He wants you to turn your thoughts toward Him throughout the day. He longs for you to ask Him for help – for yourself, for the people around you, for the world. He wants to visit with you, right where you are now.

Brothers and sisters, we are not afraid to enter the most Holy Room. We enter boldly because of the blood of Jesus. His way is new because He lives. It has been opened for us through the curtain. I'm talking about His body.

We also have a great priest over the house of God. So let us come near to God with a sincere heart. Let us come near boldly because of our faith. Our hearts have been sprinkled. Our minds have been cleansed from a sense of guilt. Our bodies have been washed with pure water.

Let us hold firmly to the hope we claim to have. The God who promised is faithful.–Hebrews 10

So put on all of God's armor. Evil days will come. But you will be able to stand up to anything. And after you have done everything you can, you will still be standing.

So remain strong in the faith. Put the belt of truth around your waist. Put the armor of godliness on your chest. Wear on your feet what will prepare you to tell the good news of peace. Also, pick up the shield of faith. With it you can put out all the flaming arrows of the evil one. Put on the helmet of salvation; and take the sword of the Holy Spirit – the sword is God's Word.

At all times, pray by the power of the Spirit. Pray all kinds of prayers. Be watchful, so that you can pray. Always keep on praying for all the Lord's people.

There's true power in the number seven. I call this the law of attack and defense in the spiritual realm.

Attack # 1: Lies about God, His love for you, and His final victory.

Your Defense: The Truth

God is the source of all truth. He has chosen to give you real knowledge of Himself and his salvation for you. By holding firmly to the truth He has shown you, especially in the Bible, you can defeat the lies of satan.

Attack # 2: Temptations to ignore God's direction for living; you are invited to enjoy so many sinful pleasures. "After all, how could it hurt? Choose your own lifestyle. Decide your own values. Don't let anyone judge you. Satisfy your desires."

Your Defense: Godliness

God Himself protects you with the righteousness of Christ. The Spirit who is Holy lives in you; to help you live a clean life. Commit yourself to faithfully following His ways of wisdom. Do the right thing.

Attack # 3: Temptations to believe that God's ways do not work

You will hear so-called practical advice about how to get things done in the real world. "Don't let anyone stand in your way. Do what it takes to get what you want. Watch out for yourself, nobody else will."

Your Defense: The Good News of Peace

The ways of force and violence turn back on those who use them. But the gospel of peace has power to change lives. It works. The good news from God is that His peace will overcome. Let His peace rule in your life.

Attack # 4: Arrows of doubt about God's promises in the world where science rules and machines work wonders, it can be hard to believe. "Where is the God of Heaven? If Jesus is coming, why has He taken so long? Show me. Prove it."

Your Defense: Faith

Faith is a true gift of God. By this gift you can be sure of what you hope for in Jesus. You can be certain of God even though you cannot see Him. Learn to see in a new way with the eyes of faith. Trust the God who has already done so much for you.

Attack # 5: Bringing charges against you to produce feelings of guilt.

You are attacked again and again by reminders of your sin. "You blew it. You always fail. What is the matter with you? God could never use someone like you!"

Your Defense: Understanding your Salvation

God has taken care of your sin once and for all through the cross of Jesus. Your salvation in Jesus is firm and cannot be lost. God has already given you a role to play in His Kingdom. Go forward with God. Be sure of His power to defeat your sin.

Attack # 6: Things that distract you and keep you from growing in God

You are tempted not to read the Bible. It is so easy to fill up your time with other things. "It's just a old book with other people's religious opinions. It's hard to read. You have more important things to do. Take a break. Read it later.

Your Defense: The Word of God

God has given you a strong and active weapon in His Word. It is not just words on a page, but His mighty Word that does what He wants it to. The Bible is the Word of God. God will speak to you through it. Read it every day. Study it carefully. Know it deeply. Let it work God's purposes in you and for you.

Attack # 7: Anything to keep you away from God

Satan wants you to forget about God, to believe what God really does not make any difference in the world.

"Can't you admit that it is impossible to talk to Him? How silly to think God hears or cares about what you say."

Your Defense: Prayer

Because of your relationship with Jesus you can come right into the presence of your Father. You can freely and openly talk to Him, share with Him, cry out to Him. The very reason God made you was to have this kind of close fellowship with Him. Pray all the time. Your love for God will grow deep; and you will be amazed at what God will do.

The Final Word –

Everyone who believes that Jesus is the Christ is a child of God. And everyone who loves the Father loves His children as well.

Here is how we know that we love God's children. We know it when we love God and obey His commands. In fact, here is what it means to love God. We love Him by obeying His commands; and His commands are not hard to obey. That's because everyone who is a child of God has won the battle over the world. Our faith has won the battle for us. Who is it that has won the battle over the world? Only the person who believed that Jesus is the Son of God. – 1 John 5

Note section for readers

WRITE IT DOWN

_____

_____

_____

_____

_____

_____

_____

_____

_____

_____

_____

Blueprint Eight

How Can I find courage?

The shelter of God's presence

First, remember that showing courage is not the same as having a bad attitude or acting tough. Real courage is having the strength and boldness to do what is right, even when it is hard. It is standing up for and acting on what you believe to be good and true.

Courage is possible only when you are sure of what you believe. Put your trust in God – you cannot be more sure of anything than Him. He will give you a spirit of power and confidence – real courage.

The good book of Psalm, Chapter 27, is one of my favorite songs on courage.

The Lord is my light, and He saves me.
Why should I fear anyone?
The Lord is my place of safety.
Why should I be afraid?
My enemies are evil.
They will trip and fall when they attack me and try to swallow me up.

"Can't you admit that it is impossible to talk to Him? How silly to think God hears or cares about what you say."

Your Defense: Prayer

Because of your relationship with Jesus you can come right into the presence of your Father. You can freely and openly talk to Him, share with Him, cry out to Him. The very reason God made you was to have this kind of close fellowship with Him. Pray all the time. Your love for God will grow deep; and you will be amazed at what God will do.

The Final Word

Everyone who believes that Jesus is the Christ is a child of God. And everyone who loves the Father loves His children as well.

Here is how we know that we love God's children. We know it when we love God's children. We know it when we love God and obey His commands. In fact, here is what it means to love God. We love Him by obeying His commands. And His commands are not hard to obey. That's because everyone who is a child of God has won the battle over the world. Our faith has won the battle for us. Who is it that has won the battle over the world? The person who believes Jesus is the Son of God. – 1 John 5

Even if an army attacks me, my heart will not be afraid. Even if war breaks out against me. I will still trust in God.

Courage comes from trusting God. It can't be mentally drummed up. It comes from believing what God says regardless of what the circumstances look like. Courage comes from faith. Where does discouragement come from? From fear and unbelief. It comes when you listen to the devil's lies about what God is not going to do for you. As the people of God, you and I must shake off discouragement and rise up with courage. We must quit looking at our own abilities and failures and limitations and start looking to God. We must rise up in the name of Jesus and the power of His spirit and establish the kingdom of heaven upon earth.

If you've been discouraged lately, stop listening to the enemies lies. Stop receiving such evil reports. Whenever someone tells you God is not going to deliver you, you just tell them, "He's already delivered me in the name of Jesus." Once you begin to realize who you are and what you've been given by the power of God, you'll quit letting the devil run all over you. God didn't suggest that you be strong and courageous. That is His command.

In the book of Joshua, Joshua becomes Israel's leader. It states in Joshua, Chapter 1, verses 1-9; "Moses, the servant of the Lord, died. After that, the Lord spoke to Joshua, the son of Nun. Joshua was Moses' helper. The Lord said to Joshua, "My servant Moses is dead. Now then, I want you and all these people to get ready to go across the Jordan River. I want all of you to go into the land I am about to give to the Israelites. I will give all of you every place you walk on, just as I promised Moses. Your territory will reach from the Negev Desert all the way to Lebanon. The great Euphrates River will be to the east. The Mediterranean Sea will be to the west. Your territory will include all the Hittite country.

Joshua, no one will be able to oppose you as long as you live. I will be with you, just as I was with Moses. I will never leave you. I will never desert you. Be strong and brave. You will lead these people. They will take the land as their very own. It is the land I promised to give their people of long ago. Be strong and very brave. Make sure you obey the whole law my servant Moses gave you. Do not turn away from it to the right or the left.

Then you will have success everywhere you go. Never stop reading this Book of the Law. Day and night you must think about what it says. Make sure you do everything written in it. Then things will go well with you. And you will have great success. Here is what I am commanding you to do. Be strong and brave. Do not be afraid. Do not lose hope. I am the Lord your God. I will be with you everywhere you go."

Storms are coming. Find shelter. Another essential topic I would like to touch on is the shelter of God's presence. Hardly a day goes by that I don't check the weather app on my phone. Why? I want to know what I might face today. I want to be prepared for sunshine or rain, powdery snow or ice on the roads, clear skies or a tornado.

I wish I had an app that would give me a different kind of forecast. I need an app that will give me the forecast for the real storms of my life – the storms in relationships, temptations, trouble at work, and the general chaos of the daily grind. Unfortunately, no such app exists. Instead, we typically put one foot in front of the other and slog through each day as it comes.

But we don't have to live that way. We know two things for sure about the storms of life.

1. Storms are going to happen.
2. We're never alone, even when life assaults us with all of its brutality.

I'm ecstatic you're taking this journey with me as we study a few Psalms – ancient worship songs – to learn where God is and what God is doing in the middle of our storms. At times we may feel like asking, "Where is God when life is hard?" There are very important answers to that question, as the Psalmist will help us see. But this study offers more than just information about God. The shelter of God's presence located throughout the good book of Psalms will also help you answer the question, "Where do I go when life gets tough?" Let's learn to live in the middle of the ancient lyrics, these wonderful psalms. Let's encounter the truth that God does show up personally in our lives, no matter what storm comes our way. He is our storm shelter.

Living a life of faith takes courage. Most people don't realize it, but it does. It takes courage to stand up in the face of sickness and declare you're healed by the stripes of Jesus.

Then you will have success everywhere you go. Never stop reading this Book of the Law. Day and night you must think about what it says. Make sure you do everything written in it. Then things will go well with you. And you will have great success. Here is what I commanding you to do. Be strong and brave. Do not be afraid. Do not lose hope. I am the Lord your God. I will be with you everywhere you go.

Storms are coming. Find shelter. Another essential topic I would like to touch on is the shelter of God's presence. Hardly a day goes by that I don't check the weather app on my phone. Why? I want to know what I might face today. I want to be prepared for sunshine or rain, powdery snow or ice on the roads, clear skies or a tornado.

I wish I had an app that would give me a different kind of forecast. I need an app that will give me the forecast for the real storms of my life – the storms in relationships, temptations, trouble at work, and the general chaos of the daily grind. Unfortunately, no such app exists. Instead, we typically put one foot in front of the other and slog through each day as it comes.

It takes courage to believe for prosperity and put your last dime in the offering plate when poverty is staring you in the face. There are going to be some days when you'd rather pull the covers over your head and hide than take another faith stand against the devil. But you can't; because the battle of faith isn't fought once and then forgotten. If you want to live in victory, you have to fight it again and again.

There's no way around it. Of course, some of God's people still try to find one. The Israelites, for example, thought their battles should be over when they crossed the Red Sea. So when they heard reports of giants living in the Promised Land, they decided they couldn't face the fight. Their courage failed them. So they took a 40 year detour through the wilderness. But you know what? They still couldn't avoid that fight. When the time came for the next generation to enter the Promised Land, the giants were still there.

This time, however, they found the courage to face them. Where did they find it? In the Word of God. Their leader, Joshua, had obeyed the instruction of the Lord and kept that Word on his mind and in his heart day and night.

He meditated on it and let it constantly remind him that God was on their side.

If you're going to fight the good fight of faith to the finish, you'll have to do just like Joshua did. You'll have to continually draw courage from the Word of God. So make up your mind to do it. Get into that Word and let it change you from a coward to an overcomer. Then march into battle and slay the giants in your land.

Note section for readers

WRITE IT DOWN

Blueprint Nine

The Believer's Authority

God wants His people to have order in their lives. He made the world with different authorities to help things run smoothly. God wants those with authority – those in the home, the workplace, the government, and His church – to be His servants for good.

God does not want people to rebel against what He Himself has set up. However, God's people must remember that the final authority is always God himself. If those with power do not honor God, the followers of Jesus will sometimes have to obey God rather than men.

All of you must obey those who rule over you. There are no authorities except the ones God has chosen. Those who now rule have been chosen by God. So whoever opposes the authorities opposes leaders whom God has appointed. Those who do that will be judged. If you do what is right, you won't need to be afraid of your rulers. But watch out if you do what is wrong. You don't want to be afraid of those in authority, do you? Then do what is right, and you will be praised. – Romans 13

Even though satan lost all his authority on this earth the day Jesus rose from the dead, for the past 2,000 years he's been running around as a spiritual outlaw – continuing to kill, steal from and destroy all who will let him. But, you know, he's not going to be able to do that much longer. There's coming a day when he's going to be put out of business completely. There's coming a day when the evil he's done here on earth will be put totally underfoot by the power of God.

Jesus is the Head of the church. You and I are the feet. We are the ones who are going to take His authority and power and stomp on sin and sickness and every other demonic thing in this earth. We are the ones God is going to use, as Acts 2:35 says to make Jesus' enemies His footstool.

That's what Jesus was telling us when He said, "Go ye into all the world, and preach the gospel to every creature...cast out devils...lay hands on the sick" – Mark 16: 15-18. He was saying, "Go ye and be My foot." He was saying, "All power and authority has been given unto Me, both in heaven and on earth. Therefore you take it and use it to put the devil under." But instead of obeying Him, we've waited around wondering when God was going to do something about this mess here on earth. We've sat around wondering why it's taking so long for Jesus to come back.

We're the reason it's taking so long. Jesus is waiting on you and me. He's waiting on us to step out in His power, put the devil in his place, and win the world. He's waiting on us to drop our silly doctrinal differences and get busy doing what God wants us to do.

The Bible says that one can put a thousand to flight and two can put 10,000 to flight. Every time we get together, we increase our strength astronomically.

If we'd just get together and figure out who we are, if we'd realize that we're the feet of Jesus, we could kick satan out of earth's affairs with ease.

"But [Christ Jesus] made Himself of no reputation and took upon Him the form of a servant, and was made in the likeness of men." This powerful verse is located in the book of Philippians 2:7. I'm going to do my best to break it down to you all because this information is vital. The truth of this verse hasn't really dawned on most people. They mistakenly think that Jesus was able to work wonders, to perform miracles, and to live above sin because He had divine powers that we don't have. Thus, they have never really aspired to live like He lived.

What us humans, spiritual humans, fail to realize is that when Jesus came to earth, He voluntarily gave up that advantage, living His life here not as God but as a man. He had no innate supernatural powers. He had no ability to perform miracles until after He was anointed by the Holy Spirit as recorded in Luke 4, Acts 10:38.

He worked wonders, not by His own power but by the power of the Father, saying, "The Father that dwelleth in Me, He doeth the works" – John 14:10

And when He prayed, He prayed not as a divine One who had authority as God, but as a man who walked obediently with God. And, as Hebrews 5:7 says, His prayers were heard not because of His deity, but "because of His reverence toward God." Jesus, the divine Son of God, set aside the privileges and powers of deity for a time and lived as a man on earth. Once you grasp that, it will absolutely thrill your soul. Why? Because it means that you, as a reborn child of God, filled with the same Holy Spirit as Jesus was, have the same opportunity to live as He lived on earth. In fact, that is exactly what He intends. In John 17:18 He said to the Father, "Just as You sent Men into the world, I have also sent them into the world." He's given you the ability and the command to live above sin, to live in fellowship with the Father, to preach the gospel, to heal the sick, to raise the dead, to cast out demons and to make disciples.

Once you realize that, you'll throw off the shackles of doubt that have held you back. You'll begin to live as Jesus meant for you to live – not as a sin-ridden son of fallen man, but as a reborn child of the Most High God. Then those around you will actually begin to see Jesus – in you.

In Psalm 18:37-38 it states, "I have pursued mine enemies and overtaken them...they are fallen under my feet."

You hold the keys. If you've been standing around wringing your hands and worrying about what the devil is doing, it's time you made a switch. It's time you put that devil under your feet. Jesus has already given you all the power and authority you need to do it. He's given you the keys of the kingdom. He's promised you that whatever you declare locked on earth is locked in heaven and whatever you declare unlocked on earth is unlocked in the heavenlies – Matthew 16:19. That means you can speak the Word and bind wicked spirits. You can speak the Word and loose the angelic forces of God to work in your behalf.

What's more, you've been given the power of attorney that enables you to use the mighty Name of Jesus; a name that's above every other name; a name which will cause every knee to bow – in heaven, in earth, and under the earth. – Philippians 2:9-10

So, don't waste time worrying about the devil. Take authority over him. Bind the evil spirits that are trying to destroy your home, your church and your nation. Loose God's Word in the earth and enforce it with the name of Jesus.

You hold the keys. Learn to use them and before long the devil will be wringing his hands worrying about you!

Note section for readers

WRITE IT DOWN

_____

_____

Blueprint Ten

Freedom from fear

God is out ultimate protection. Why do we fear? "He hath said, I will never leave thee, no forsake thee. So that we may boldly say, The Lord is my helper, and I will not fear what man shall do unto me." – Hebrews 13: 5-6

Self-Consciousness is a major problem in the Body of Christ today. It keeps us from doing the things God tells us to do. Instead of simply obeying Him, it makes us start to wonder,

"Now what will people think of me if I do that?"

"What if I command that person to get out of the wheelchair and he doesn't get up?"

"What if I start believing for prosperity and go broke?"

"What about that, God?"

"I won't look too good will I?"

If you've ever been through that, let me tell you something; it doesn't matter how you look. It's that you obey God that counts. When it comes to obeying God, your own reputation doesn't count. And, the sooner you forget it the better off you'll be. But you know what's ironic? Once you do that your reputation gets better. It's a funny thing. When you lose that desire to protect your image, your image will improve. Why? Because then, when people look at you, instead of seeing that puny little image you have of yourself, they'll see the image of the Lord Jesus coming through.

So put aside that old self-consciousness and develop God-consciousness instead. Stop being dominated by the fear of man and start being motivated by faith in what Jesus can do. After all, He has promised He will never leave you nor forsake you. Grab hold of that. Believe it. Act on it. Once you do, you'll realize there's really nothing to be afraid of anymore.

What would you think if I told you that you could live without fear?

Will you believe me if I said despite what you saw on the news this morning or tonight; you could be perfectly at peace? Impossible? Unrealistic? NO!

You see, fear isn't just a reaction to external circumstances. It's a spiritual force. It begins inside of you. And it is totally destructive. In fact, fear is satan's primary weapon. He moves in response to faith. He challenges the promises of God with it.

An excellent example of this is found in Matthew 14 when Jesus invited Peter to come to Him on the water. "But when he (Peter) saw the wind boisterous, he was afraid; and beginning to sink, he cried, saying, Lord, save me" – verse 30. What enabled Peter to walk on the water? His faith in the Word of Jesus. What caused to sink, though? He saw the wind boisterous and was afraid. It wasn't the wind that defeated him; it was the fear of it. He looked at his circumstances, gave in to the fear, and the result was defeat. If Peter had kept his focus on Jesus, his faith would never have wavered. All the blustering and blowing in the world couldn't have drawn him off course.

Faith is developed by meditating on God's Word. Fear is developed by meditating on satan's lies. Such fearful meditation is called "worrying". Don't do it. The Word of God is the sword of the spirit. Use it to fight satan every time he comes against you. Hold up your shield of faith and quench all of his fiery darts. Speak words of faith and fear will depart.

The Bible Meets Life

Know any "helicopter parents"? You've probably seen some. There are the moms and dads who hover obsessively over their children, afraid they might scrape a knee, need assistance, or get hurt feelings. Love is certainly a motive behind such behavior, but so is fear. And either way, the children will still fall down.

Many of us "hover" over ourselves, as well. We try to prevent any negative experiences from coming our way. Often we cross the line between protecting ourselves and living in fear. How do we find that line? How do we balance between living in unhealthy fear and living with total disregard for the threats that challenge us? Such balance is gained through trust in God's protection.

No matter what we face, we can know God is present.

Psalm 91 points us toward an awareness of God's presence. The Psalmist helps us see that, while we don't need to live recklessly, we also don't need to live in fear. God is the great Hero of our story, and we can rely on Him for ultimate protection.

What does the Bible say?

Psalm 91:1-4, 9-11, 14-16

1. The one who lives under the protection of the Most High dwells in the shadow of the Almighty.
2. I will say to the Lord, "My refuge and my fortress, my God, in whom I trust."
3. He Himself will deliver you from the hunter's net, from the destructive plague.
4. He will cover you with his feathers; you will take refuge under His wings. His faithfulness will be a protective shield.
9. Because you have made the Lord – my refuge, the Most High – your dwelling place,

10. no harm will come to you; no plague will come near your tent.

11. For He will give His angels orders concerning you, to protect you in all your ways.

14. Because He is lovingly devoted to me, I will deliver him; I will protect him because he knows My name.

15. When He calls out to me, I will answer Him; I will be with him in trouble. I will rescue him and give him honor.

16. I will satisfy him with a long life and show him My salvation.

We think it was Benjamin Franklin who first said, "Nothing is certain except death and taxes." He made a good point. Finding something meaningful to count on in life often seems like a fool's errand. Jobs come and go. People let us down. Our stuff breaks. We even let ourselves down. But then God enters the picture. Nothing in this world can compare with the strength and protection God gives us. He is certain.

One way we can begin to understand just how God works on our behalf is to investigate the names and titles He uses to reveal Himself. Notice these examples from verses 1-2:

1. The Most High. No one is above God. He is the One who stands in the loftiest position. He is supreme.

2. Almighty. This is not just "stronger-than-the-next guy" strength. God holds all the power in all of creation throughout all of eternity.

3. Lord. This is the name that God used to reveal Himself to His chosen people. It is the covenant name Yahweh, which means "I am". In other words, God is self-existent, self-sustaining, and eternal. He is the one who creates and holds everything else together.

When we see God in light of how He reveals Himself, counting on Him for protection suddenly becomes a lot easier. Also notice God's hospitality in these verses. We're under His protection, in His shadow, in His fortress, and under His wing. The great God of the universe – who doesn't need me, you, or anyone else – does something completely unnecessary and perhaps unexpected; He welcomes us into His protective presence.

In the movie "The Wizard of Oz", Dorothy, the Tin Man, and the Scarecrow were traveling down the Yellow Brick Road when the Tin Man explained the dangers that might lurk ahead. The three of them began to chant over and over again "Lions and tigers and bear, Oh my!"

Chapter 91, verses 3-13, the Psalmist painted his own picture of the dangers that lurk in the shadowy places of our lives; the hunter's net, the destructive plague, the terror of the night, the arrow that flies by day, the plague that stalks in darkness, the pestilence that ravages at noon, the lion, the cobra, and so on.

If that weren't enough, we often rehearse our own secret fears – both the real problems we face and the perceived dangers we fear may be lurking in the shadows. Physical pain. Mental stress. Emotional struggle. Financial worry. If we're not careful, we'll find ourselves chanting our own version of "Lions and tigers and bears, oh my!"

I don't say that to trivialize your problems. But the truth is you have someone watching over you who is greater than those problems. God's sovereignty means He can protect you in all things.

God goes so far as to involve the very forces of heaven on your behalf "to protect you in all your ways." Our Heavenly Father is absolutely, positively certain you never will be in any circumstance in which He is not watching you, guarding you, and guiding you. You will run into problems, of course – but you won't be alone. God's kind control means His eye is on you.

Psalm 91: 14-16

God is fully able to protect us. But He places a decision in our laps – the decision to be devoted to Him or to rely on ourselves.

1. God knows your name. You are not anonymous to the King of the universe. He knows you personally. – Isaiah 49:16

2. God knows when you call out to Him. In the midst of countless prayers lifted up before Him, God hears your prayer. And He listens. – 1 John 5:14-15

3. God is right beside you when trouble appears. The idea that God would leave you as an orphan is an outright lie. He never abandons His people. – Joshua 1:9, Matthew 28:20

4. God rescues and honors you. Most people in trouble would be happy just to be rescued and taken out of danger. But God replaces the hazards with a place of honor. God doesn't just want you sheltered; he wants you satisfied with eternal salvation. – Ephesians 2:7-9

Best of all, God wants you to have an eternal relationship with Him through the power of Jesus' sacrifice for us. When you've made the decision to lovingly surrender to His grace and mercy, then the dangers, turmoil, and chaos of life lose their teeth. They become just more opportunities for God to show off how much He loves you.

As you hear from God in the days to come, use the space below to record His answers to your prayer.

Note section for readers

WRITE IT DOWN

Blueprint Eleven

The company you keep

"It is better to be alone, than in the wrong company"
A Small Meditation Break from the Author

Tell me who your best friends are, and I will tell you who you are. If you run with wolves you will learn how to howl. But, if you associate with eagles, you will learn how to soar to great heights. "A mirror reflects a man's face, but what he is really like is shown by the kind of friends he chooses." The simple but true fact of life is that you become like those with whom you closely associate – "for the good and the bad."

The less you associate with some people, the more your life will improve. Any time you tolerate "mediocrity in others, it increases your mediocrity." An important attribute in successful people is their impatience with negative thinking and negative acting people. As you grow, your associates will change. Some of your friends will not want you to go on. "They will want you to stay where they are." Friends that don't help you climb will want you to crawl. "Your friends will stretch your vision or choke your dream." Those that don't increase you will eventually decrease you. Consider this:

- Never receive counsel from unproductive people.
- Never discuss your problems with someone incapable of contributing to the solution, because those who never succeed themselves are always first to tell you how. Not everyone has a right to speak into your life. You are certain to get the worst of the bargain when you exchange ideas with the wrong people.
- "Don't follow anyone who's not going anywhere." With some people you spend an evening; with others you invest in it.
- Be careful where you stop to inquire for directions along the road of life.
- "Wise is the person who fortifies his life with the right friendships."

Happy moments...praise God

Difficult moments...seek God

Quiet moments...worship God

Painful moments...trust God

Every moment...thank God

If you see people without a smile today...give them one of yours.

Your best friend is your Lord Jesus Christ. One of my favorite descriptions of a genuine relationship with God was in a book I read by one of my favorite authors, James P. Gills. It's called a "Delicate Balance with the Creator".

Knowledge. Covenant. Worship. Three vital elements that comprise an ideal relationship between creation and creator. "Value of Three" triangle that makes up an ideal relationship with God.

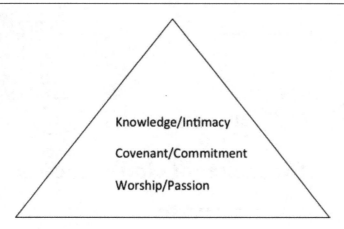

1. Intimacy – On the emotional side of the love triangle lies intimacy, or "knowing"- in both Hebrew and Greek, "to know" implies an intimate relationship best seen in a very close friendship.
2. Commitment – the cognizant side of the love triangle. That's the "down-to-brass-tacks" loyalty in a marital relationship. It provides the reliable strength necessary for the relationship to survive all the ups and downs of life.
3. Passion – On the motivational side of the triangle we find the passion level in a relationship. Passion cements the whole relationship into one cohesive bond.

Note section for readers

WRITE IT DOWN

_____

_____

_____

_____

Blueprint Twelve

The shelter of God's peace

Do you make New Year resolutions? If not, you still know which resolutions are most common: exercise, lose weight, spend more time with family, read more, watch less TV, and so on.

Have you ever thought about why people make such resolutions? One of the main reasons is a desire for a calmer life. We think, "If I can just live better, eat better, and be a better family member, then life will take on a new sense of harmony." Or, "If I can just gain a sense of balance or control, I will have a more peaceful life." But then life happens, and the idea of a better anything gets shot to pieces.

In reality, we don't need better resolutions. We need a revolution. That's because resolutions are based on our ability to change our circumstances. A revolution is based on allowing a new authority to take charge and transform us. We need the revolutionary presence of God to bring to us what we cannot produce on our own.

Peace, even in the midst of life's turmoil, is one of the revolutionary results of God's presence in our lives.

<u>What does the Bible say?</u> Psalm 46: 1-11

1. God is our refuge and strength, a helper who is always found in times of trouble.
2. Therefore we will not be afraid, though the earth trembles and the mountains topple into the depths of the seas,
3. though its waters roar and foam and the mountains quake with its turmoil.
4. There is a river – its streams delight the city of God, the holy dwelling place of the Most High.
5. God is within her; she will not be toppled. God will help her when the morning dawns.
6. Nations rage, kingdoms topple; the earth melts when He lifts His voice.
7. The Lord of Hosts is with us; the God of Jacob is our stronghold.
8. Come; see the works of the Lord, who brings devastation on the earth.
9. He makes wars cease throughout the earth. He shatters bows and cuts spears to pieces; He burns up the chariots.
10. "Stop your fighting – and know that I am God, exalted among the nations, exalted on the earth."
11. Yahweh of Hosts is with us; the God of Jacob is our stronghold.

"And let the peace (soul harmony which comes) from Christ rule (act as umpire continually) in your hearts [deciding and settling with finality all questions that arise in your minds...And be thankful (appreciative), giving praise to God always]." – Colossians 3:15

Have you been praying that God will let you know whether a certain action you want to take is agreeable to His will or not? Let the peace of Christ be your guide.

Let it help you settle the issue. If you start to take that action and you realize you don't have peace about it, don't do it.

Remember, though, that this inner leading of the Holy Spirit, the subtle sense of uneasiness or peace He gives you, is something you have to watch and listen for carefully. He generally won't just come up and knock you out of one beg one morning and tell you what you need to do. The primary way He speaks to you is by what the Bible calls an inward witness.

So, you have to listen. You can't just stay busy about the things of the world all the time. You have to give Him time and attention.

Also, watch out for strife. If you're irritated and upset about things in your life, it will be very hard to receive that quiet guidance from the Holy Spirit. So take heed to the instructions at the end of this scripture and "be thankful...appreciative, giving praise to God always." Maintain a thankful, grateful heart. You'll find it much easier to hear the "umpire of peace" when He makes a call.

Peace has all sorts of definitions. For some people, peace is the absence of open hostility toward me. For others, peace is only present when everyone lives in perfect harmony with one another. My guess is that most of us would settle for something in the middle – something that applies to our everyday lives. Peace for me would mean fewer surprises at work, less stress in my family, and enough money to pay my bills. Is that too much to ask?

Psalm 46 points to a peace that goes way beyond simply overcoming the rut of daily routines. It's a change God brings that no calamity can overwhelm. How God does this is wrapped up in His very person.

Notice how the Psalmist began verse 1 in Psalm 46: "God is...
"Those might be the two most powerful words you can read, hear, or speak. Next, the Psalmist described God with three distinct terms.

1. Refuge. When God is our refuge, we have a place to hide when life assaults us. When you feel battered and bruised and bullied, you can find a place of shelter with your Heavenly Father.

2. Strength. When life is hard, we're not forced to continue in our own power. Rather, God empowers us to take on life no matter what comes our way.

3. Helper. God is always there to help us. I love how personal this is. God, the Creator and Master of all things, helps me. No matter what I face, God is personally there to help.

The Psalmist also described some pretty serious threats. We may not be physically facing an earthquake, mountains toppling into the sea, or the ocean flooding over us – but sometimes it feels like we are. We can't seem to get our footing. Stuff is crashing down all around us. Troubles show up like a flood against us. But the one who trusts in God does not have to be afraid.

Words have enormous power. A word from our enemy can remove our sense of peace and replace it with anxiety in a split second. The voice of God, though, is far greater. When He speaks, His words confront those who oppose His peace. When God speaks, all the enemies of peace are rendered null and void.

It comes down to a choice. God has made peace possible between Himself and us. We were the enemies raging against His Kingdom. We were the rebels making alliances with the chaos of the world. But God stands infinitely over and above all things. He is the true Hero of our battle, and He offers peace. But we must choose to trust Jesus rather than our stuff and our own will power.

Yahweh is our stronghold. The name Yahweh is the ancient Hebrew name God used to reveal Himself as "the great I AM." It signals to us that

He is eternal and needs nothing to sustain Him. Peace is ours because no nation, no act of humanity, and no self-imposed gain is greater than our God.

You need God's presence that brings peace in all kinds of situations:

- When family comes to visit.
- When the project at work is coming apart at the seams.
- When it's Saturday and your teenage daughter is an hour and a half late coming home – and she won't answer her phone.
- When you're enticed or tempted to sin for what seems like the millionth time.
- When problems must be solved, relationships must be mended, and chaos rages around you.

God's presence and peace is what you need, and God provides them. God is simply waiting for you to rush into His stronghold. The door is always open.

Consider the following suggestions for allowing God to work in your life and bring peace:

- Dwell in God's Word. Read Psalm 46 daily for the next week. Choose one verse to memorize so you can remind yourself about God's power during times of turmoil.
- Take a retreat. Spend a significant portion of time alone in prayer and worship this week. Ask God to give you peace.
- Get involved. Identify a group or ministry that seeks to bring spiritual peace into the lives of people. Determine how you can help that cause.

You're going to face turmoil every day. That's not a pleasant reality, but it's time. Fortunately, you can actively choose to make a resolution in the face of turmoil. Be intentional to let God work a revolution in your life – a revolution of His peace and presence.

Note section for readers

WRITE IT DOWN

_____

_____

_____

_____

_____

_____

_____

_____

_____

_____

_____

Blueprint Thirteen

Bad feelings about the past

"...But this one thing I do, forgetting those things which are behind, and reaching forth unto those things with are before." – Philippians 3:13

Failures and disappointments. Aches and pains from the past that just won't seem to go away. Most of us know what it's like to suffer from them but too few of us know what it's like to suffer from them; but too few of us know just what to do about them. So we limp along, hoping somehow they'll magically stop hurting. But it never happens that way. In fact, the passing of time often leaves us in worse condition – not better. Because, instead of putting those painful failures behind us, we often dwell on them until they become more real to us than the promises of God. We focus on them until we become bogged down in depression, frozen in our tracks by the fear that if we go on, we'll only fail again.

Forget about those failures of the past. That's what God has done – Hebrews 8:12. And if He doesn't remember them anymore, why should you? The Bible says God's mercies are new every morning. So if you'll take God at His word, you can wake up every morning to a brand-new world. You can live life totally unhindered by the past.

So, do it. Replace thoughts of yesterday's mistakes with scriptural promises about your future. As you do that, hope will start taking the place of depression. The spiritual aches and pains that have crippled you for so long will quickly disappear. Instead of looking behind you and saying, "I can't," you'll begin to look ahead and say, "I can do all things through Christ which strengthens me."

First, you need to know that God made you. This means that your own conscience will help you keep track of the right and wrong things you have done. It is natural for you to feel the guilt of your wrong actions. This is a first step toward getting yourself right with God and with others.

You must openly admit to the wrong things you have done. Tell God you are sorry for them. Do what you can to set things right with other people. Then trust God to forgive you and believe that He can set you free inside. Because of what Jesus has done for you, God can bring you a new beginning, a new life.

Blessed is the person whose lawless acts are forgiven.
Their sins have been taken away.
Blessed is the person whose sin the Lord never counts against them.
That person doesn't want to cheat anymore.
I admitted my sin to you.
I didn't cover up the wrong I had done.
I said, "I will admit my lawless acts to the Lord."
And you forgave the guilt of my sin–Psalm 32

We limp along, hoping somehow those hidden wounds will magically stop hurting; thinking that maybe (with a little extra sleep or an extra helping of dessert) that nagging sense of depression will finally disappear. But does it ever happen that way? No. I know. I've been there.

But thank God, I'm not there anymore. You see, over the past few years, I've faced some fierce spiritual battles. And I've found out those battles can leave you bruised and beaten up on the inside just as surely as a fist fight can leave you bruised and beaten up on the outside.

Before I was born again, I learned just how physically devastating a real slug-it-out kind of brawl could be. Yet as bad as I felt, a few days rest would take care of me. The healing of a bruised and beaten spirit, however, doesn't come that easily. In fact, the passing of time often worsens this condition.

But there is a way out. If depression has put you into a spiritual nose dive, all you have to do to break out of it is to get your eyes off the past and onto your future – a future that's been guaranteed by Christ Jesus through the exceeding great and precious promises in His word.

Chances are that won't come easily to you at first. Your mind has probably had years of practice in focusing on the past. Like an old horse that habitually heads for the barn, your thoughts will probably start galloping in that direction every time you give them any slack.

So, don't give them that slack. Keep the reign tight. Purposely meditate on the Word of God.

Replace thoughts of the past with scriptural promises about your future and be diligent about it. Then, instead of being a wounded soldier, you'll become the conquering warrior God made you to be.

Note section for readers

WRITE IT DOWN

Blueprint Fourteen

If God will forgive me, can I do whatever I please?

The cross of Jesus takes away the penalty of our wrongdoing. God's forgiveness is freely offered to you, but it is not cheap. It cost God His only Son. And if we abuse this gift and fail to follow and obey God's risen Son, then no sacrifice for sins is left. The power of God's forgiveness frees you to do what is right, not to return to the empty and deadly life of sin.

"Here is the message we have heard from Him and announce to you. God is light. There is no darkness in Him at all. Suppose we say that we share life with God but still walk in darkness. Then we are lying. We are not living out the truth. But suppose we walk in the light, just as He is in the light. Then we share life with one another. And the blood of Jesus, his son, makes us pure from all sin. – 1 John 1

Have you ever tried to forgive someone...and found you simply couldn't do it? You've cried about it and prayed about it and asked God to help you, but those old feelings of resentment just failed to go away. Put an end to those kinds of failures in the future by basing your forgiveness on faith rather than feelings. True forgiveness doesn't have anything at all to do with how you feel. It's an act of the will. It is based on obedience to God and on faith in Him.

That means once you've forgiven a person, you need to consider them permanently forgiven. When old feelings rise up within you and satan tries to convince you that you haven't really forgiven them, resist him. Say, "No, I've already forgiven that person by faith. I refuse to dwell on those old feelings."

Have you ever heard anyone say, "I may forgive, but I'll never forget"? That's a second-rate kind of forgiveness that you, as a believer, are never supposed to settle for. You're to forgive supernaturally "even as God for Christ's sake hath forgiven you." You're to forgive as God forgives. To release that person from guilt permanently and unconditionally and to operate as if nothing bad ever happened between you. You're to purposely forget as well as forgive.

As you do that, something supernatural will happen within you. The pain once caused by that incident will disappear. The power of God will wash away the effects of it and you'll be able to leave it behind you once and for all. Don't become an emotional bookkeeper, keeping careful accounts of the wrongs you have suffered. Learn to forgive and forget. It will open a whole new world of blessings for you.

You'd think the holidays would be an easy time to repair damaged relationships. After all, people are in a festive spirit, there's lots of food, and gifts are exchanged. Unfortunately, festive moods don't always translate into mending relational fences. We have this lingering hope that someone will make the first move to ask for forgiveness, but it doesn't seem to happen very often.

Forgiveness is a gift that's often hard to give. Why? Because it costs so much. The person doing the forgiving essentially forks over the whole payment; the main cost is letting go of the hurt and giving up the offense that was committed.

Forgiveness means you walk away from the judge's bench and stand united with the guilty party.

Forgiveness was costly for God, too. Jesus took our punishment, and through Him, God offers us forgiveness. No matter what we've done, God forgives. What a wonderful gift He has given us. This sense of being forgiven is no mere emotion. Psalm 27 shows us that God's forgiveness moves us to a place of restoration and joy.

Joy can feel like a rare commodity in our lives. We're constantly looking for joy in things around us that are only temporary. The truth is that joy comes from something much more durable. Real joy arrives only in the form of Jesus. He is eternal, and He changes our lives rather than just smothering us with temporary gifts.

Remember that happiness can show up because the right chemicals in our brain combine or the right circumstances in our lives occur. Joy is not dependent on the temporary, but on the eternal. It's the response of our souls when we encounter God. Joy comes when our sins are forgiven and our relationship with God is restored.

Have you ever kept quiet when you knew you needed to make a confession? Our silence eats away at us. David knew that feeling, too. During the time he refused to confess his sins, he felt like he was dying on the inside.

He had the sense his bones were groaning and breaking. And it was constant – it was "day and night."

We come under the hand of God's conviction for the simple reason that He loves us. God wants us to confess our sins because confession brings about two major blessings. First, the sin itself is removed.

David wrote in another Psalm: "As far as the east is from the west, so far has He removed our transgressions from us" – Psalm 103:12. Second, the weight of conviction is removed; God lifts the foreboding feeling that our life is wasting away.

Let me give you some practical suggestions for getting better at confession sin:

- Review the day. Set aside a time each day to allow God's Spirit to survey your heart and show you any sins you've committed.

- Find the motive behind the sin. Oftentimes, there are deep-seated issues that cause us to commit particular sins. Allow God to show you the motive behind the action.

- Get God's view about the issue. Ask, "What has God said about this in the Bible?" True confession is agreeing with God about our actions and attitudes.

- Be specific. Don't generalize; instead, confess the individual and specific sins that the Spirit brings to mind.

- Commit to repentance. Completely turn from the sin with no desire to commit it again. Ask God for strength the next time you face temptation.

- Picture this scene in your mind: because of your sin, judgment is coming toward you like a huge tsunami. You have no place to hide. But then everything suddenly goes dry. The water disappears. More than that, the world is put into the most perfect condition you've ever seen. It's a miracle!

When we experience God's forgiveness for our sin, that's exactly what it is – a miracle. When we confess our sin to God, He removes it completely and fully restores our relationship. Once we have confessed and been forgiven, then we can live in the restored relationship offered to us by God.

This happens as we recognize the nature of God and how He acts on our behalf. David identified three ways God cares for us:

1. God is our "hiding place". We need to find protection from the very judgment we deserve. God is fully justified to pronounce His judgment on us like an absolutely overwhelming flood. After our confession, however, God Himself steps in to be the place where we find shelter.

2. God is our protection. As we live in a restored relationship with God, we don't have to fear any trouble. He removes our fear and replaces it with His joy. We still face trouble, but we're never alone.

3. God surrounds us with celebration. When others ask for our forgiveness, we often respond by forgiving in a begrudging way. Thankfully, God does nothing of the sort. He releases us from our guilt and begins celebrating.

Consider the following suggestions for seeking joy through the blessing of God's forgiveness:

- Confess. Confess any sins that plague you. Turn from them, accept God's forgiveness, and make a plan with God about how to refuse their power in your life from this point forward.

- Pray. Pray for others who have not yet experienced the joy of God's forgiveness in salvation.

- Forgive. Offer forgiveness to someone who has wronged you. (Note: You can choose to forgive even if those who harm you never ask you to do so.)

We all want the gift of joy in this life. We usually grasp for joy in the same ways we find happiness – but that won't work. Instead, choose surrender as your path to joy. Surrender your will, let go of your sin, and relish the restoration that only God can bring.

Note section for readers

WRITE IT DOWN

_____

_____

_____

_____

_____

_____

_____

_____

_____

_____

Blueprint Fifteen

Why is the world in such a mess?

Satan is a great liar and enemy of God. He came into God's good creation to destroy it. Satan blinds people to the truth. And he tries to get them to turn away from God. Sometimes people will not follow the ways of God. Then they turn the world into a place of pain, suffering and hurt.

Ever since the world was created it has been possible to see the qualities of God that are not seen. I'm talking about His eternal power and about the fact that He is God. Those things can be seen in what He has made. So people have no excuse for what they do. They knew God; but they didn't honor Him as God. They didn't thank Him. Their thinking became worthless. Their foolish hearts became dark. They claimed to be wise; but they made fools of themselves.

Faith filled words. That's what changes things. They'll move mountains into the sea. They'll turn sickness into health. They'll turn a sinner into a saint. They'll also take a sin-ridden nation and turn it into God's own country.

That's right. Then, if we believers would back up the prayers we've been praying for this nation with words of faith instead of doubt and discouragement, we'd soon begin to see spiritual resurrection in the United States and everywhere else around the world.

God promised us that if we, His people, would humble ourselves and pray and seek His face and turn from our wicked ways, He would heal our land. And let me tell you, there are prayer warriors all over this country (I hope you are one of them) who are doing what the promise requires.

But, even so, you don't hear many people saying, "This is great! God is healing the land." You don't hear people speaking out by faith the promise of God. Instead, you hear them saying, "Oh my, oh my, did you hear what those terrorists are doing?" or some other destructive thing they've seen on television.

Listen, we need to stop preaching what the terrorists are doing and start telling what God is doing. God is healing the land. We must start speaking about this country by faith instead of going around spouting bad news all the time. Of course, that will sound odd to most people. Some of them may even think we've slipped a few cogs. But that's nothing new.

Let me tell you something; one handful of believers who are listening to, trusting in and speaking out the good news of God are more powerful than all the devils on earth. One handful of believers is more powerful than a whole army of unbelieving doomsayers. The unbelief of the doomsayers will not make the faith of God of no effect.

"...The things which are impossible with men are possible with God."

Right now you and I are standing face-to-face with situations in our nation that need to be changed. Some of those situations look totally impossible. But they're not; because this country belongs to God.

He's the one who brought the United States of America into existence. He had a special purpose for it. He needed a country where the gospel could be preached freely and not suppressed.

It was God Himself who stirred the heart and mind of Christopher Columbus and planted within him the dream of charting a new course to the West. Columbus said so in his own journals "It was the Lord who put into my mind (I could feel His hand upon me) the fact that it would be possible to sail from here to the Indies. All who heard my project rejected it with laughter, ridiculing me. There's no question that the inspiration was from the Holy Spirit because He comforted me with rays of marvelous inspiration from the Holy Scriptures..."

Who brought Christopher Columbus to America? God brought him. This is God's nation. He raised it up, and it's not going to be taken away from Him.

The next time you're tempted to look at situations in this country as impossible, remember who it belongs to. Then you can discover America just like Christopher Columbus did – by faith.

Note section for readers

WRITE IT DOWN

_____

_____

_____

_____

_____

Dear Heavenly Father

Those who can potentially do the most harm to you are the predators of your heart. We all must deal with people who prey on your heart. Those are the people who enjoy taking advantage of your need to be loved and will attempt to manipulate you into doing what they want you to do. But we feel in the spirit. The spirit that personal talents, prompted by the Holy Spirit are becoming more defined within you; to help to better discern actions to take and influences you should avoid attaining God's best for you. What you do with what you have is more impressive and productive than what you have the process of creating success. People are created equal in one respect. Each person is given 24 hours each day. Great achievers and successful people are those who gain control over their time. It's not how much you do; it's how much you get done.

Disconnect from the time wasters in your life. Those who are going nowhere will hinder you from getting anywhere. Whom you associate with does matter. Small minds of unbelievers will never help perpetuate the Big Dream that God instills in you. The devil knew exactly how to entice the first man and woman. He preyed on their weakness. Your attacks will always come in areas in which you have the least strength. However, it is a constant variable of the Holy Spirit to compensate for any lack that is within you. Once this power comes to the forefront, negative spirits cease their attack.

Anytime you listen to negative talk in your life that will have you ignore God's love and His plan for you, you're being robbed of your heritage. Learn to avoid traps. Believe that I am with you my child and open all the doors to the joy you see and believe in what I've shown you. Be calm and do not let fears overcome you. Trust Me for I am the Lord who loves you. All power is Mine to give and withhold. Learn to surround yourself in my presence. You will have desire, strength, power, joy, and yes; great increase. And taking one step at a time in the right direction is the best way to cultivate your faith.

Lost Years

I may never know what it's like
To tuck my son into bed
To look at him with eyes of blue;
To hear him say, "Dad, I want
to be like you."
I will never get a chance
To see my son grow.
I've made many mistakes;
I'm sure he'll know.
During his childhood,
I won't be there for him to call,
To take him to the playground,
To teach him baseball.
I would have taken him to the lake -
Taught him to comb the lake through
In search of the biggest fish;
To find the right spot and know what to do.
All the great times we would have had.
Hayden, I'm sorry I'm not there for you.
I pray you will live for Jesus;
Any problem you have, He will see you through.

The Place

In a dark dreary prison	I had to stop talking
I learned to be free	To learn how to hear
When I looked within	When I was most afraid
I began to see	I overcame my fears
When I was alone	Sometimes I'm so happy
I met my best friend	Other times I weep
I reached my beginning	I've received all things
When I was at my end	But nothing's mine to keep
Part of me would die	I sit in perfect silence
Then I learned to live	Solace from above
Nothing left to get	All around me, hatred
I learned how to give	Deep inside me, Love

In the middle of despair, I lost all hope. Prayer was a foreign language I could not speak nor comprehend. Redemption hid itself from my understanding. Addictions dominated my past and determined my future. Inside me a black hole sucked up all light, love, and faith. Suicidal thoughts, means, and devices disabled my days and stole my nights.

Endless cycles of guilt, shame, and regret, inadequacy, and depression imprisoned me. Then heaven intervened through God's grace – love and mercy I finally realized. I must forgive myself to accept forgiveness from Him.

My remaining days will be a testimony to the life, hope and salvation found in Christ. At first, I was angry and bitter about the entire situation. I never thought it was possible to be grateful for being incarcerated, but I am. Thank God.

Because We All Wear White

Because we all wear white

You view me with a prejudice mind sight

I am seen as being less than what I am

And what I am at the very least is a human

So that should afford me at least creations minimum

But I cannot seem to get that from them

Instead I am treated with a predetermined low standard

Allowed to have no opinion so I feel like a coward

I might wear them but I am not a scrub

Outside of the place I wanted, needed, and loved

Under normal circumstances I am respected

It is this state of Georgia who thought I needed to be corrected

So here I sit grossly stereotyped

Misrepresented by inflamed media hype

At the mercy of my overseers biased assumptions

Urged to just shut up and follow their instructions

Because to them I'm the scum of the earth

Not worth the weight of afterbirth

However I am living proof that they're nowhere near right...

They just think they are because we all wear white.

Written For:

'Everyone Wearing White'

By: Christian LaSalle Walden

Who Is In Fact Wearing White

Printed in the USA
CPSIA information can be obtained
at www.ICGtesting.com
LVHW011545240124
769490LV00069B/2263